OXFORD
UNIVERSITY PRESS

Great Clarendon Street, Oxford, OX2 6DP, United Kingdom

Oxford University Press is a department of the University of Oxford. It furthers the University's objective of excellence in research, scholarship, and education by publishing worldwide. Oxford is a registered trade mark of Oxford University Press in the UK and in certain other countries

First Edition Published in 2023

British Library Cataloguing in Publication Data

Data available

ISBN: 978-1-382-04349-6

10 9 8 7 6 5 4 3

Paper used in the production of this book is a natural, recyclable product made from wood grown in sustainable forests.
The manufacturing process conforms to the environmental regulations of the country of origin.

Printed in China by Golden Cup

The manufacturer's authorised representative in the EU for product safety is Oxford University Press España S.A. of El Parque Empresarial San Fernando de Henares, Avenida de Castilla, 2 – 28830 Madrid (www.oup.es/en or product.safety@oup.com). OUP España S.A. also acts as importer into Spain of products made by the manufacturer.

Acknowledgements

The Pet Problem and *Hana's Book of Cat Facts* written by Mio Debnam

The publisher wishes to thank Heidi Clarke for their valuable contribution to the development of this book.

Content on pages 10, 41 and 42 written by Suzy Ditchburn.

Illustrated by Jennifer Jamieson and Q2A Media Services Pvt Ltd

Author photo courtesy of Mio Debnam

The publisher and author would like to thank the following for permission to use photographs and other copyright material:

Back Cover: p47(l): Issam Slimene / EyeEm / Getty Images. Photos: p45(l): GoodFocused / Shutterstock; p45(r): Eric Isselee / Shutterstock; p47(l): Issam Slimene / EyeEm / Getty Images; p47(r): MR.Yanukit / Shutterstock; p49: Nils Jacobi / Shutterstock; p52(t): ANURAK PONGPATIMET / Shutterstock; p52(bl): Drazen_ / E+ / Getty; p52(br): Linda Raymond / Moment / Getty; p53(t): Tiplyashina Evgeniya / Shutterstock; p53(b): shymar27 / Shutterstock; p55: The Art of Pics / Shutterstock; p57: Shutter Views / Shutterstock; p61: Sureeporn Teerasatean / Shutterstock; p62(l): adlaphotography / Shutterstock; p62(r): smallblackcat / Shutterstock; p63: Chris Howarth/ Namibia / Alamy Stock Photo; p64: vvvita / Shutterstock; p65: AfriPics.com / Alamy Stock Photo; p66(t): Henner Damke / Shutterstock; p66(b): Ondrej Prosicky / Shutterstock; p67(tl): Joe McDonald / Getty Images; p67(tr): mauritius images GmbH / Alamy Stock Photo; p67(b): Dennis W Donohue / Shutterstock.

Every effort has been made to contact copyright holders of material reproduced in this book. Any omissions will be rectified in subsequent printings if notice is given to the publisher.

In this book ...

Have a go!

o as in mother

g as in gem

ge as in fringe

dge as in bridge

st as in castle

ce as in prince

se as in horse

gn as in sign

kn as in knot

wr as in wrist

mb as in lamb

se as in pause

ze as in freeze

eer as in deer

ere as in sphere

ti as in solution

Read this book if ...

you want

A PET

or

to find out all about

CATS!

In this book, Hana will do whatever it takes to get a cat.

STOP AND THINK

Have you ever had a pet?
Which animal would you choose?

THE PET PROBLEM

Written by Mio Debnam
Illustrated by Jennifer Jamieson

Hana: cat lover

Gemma: ace knitter

Mum

Dad
Tasha
Fudge
Bruce
Alice: Mum's sister

Every summer, Mum's sister Alice came to stay at Hana's house. Fudge and Bruce, Alice's cats, always came with her. Hana **loved** the cats.

Her family were **NOT** so keen.

Hana's older sister Gemma didn't like the cats much.

After Alice left, Hana asked for a pet cat.

Hana **didn't** give up. She asked for a cat bed and bowl for her birthday. Instead she got …

Hana made another plan. She decided to use her pocket money.

"Lovely for lemons!" Mum said.

"The perfect place for my knitting!" Gemma cheered.

Dad nudged Hana gently.

"Listen," said Dad. "You could volunteer at the cat shelter."

"Lots of lovely cats live there!" Dad smiled.

"Good idea," said Hana.

Hana gazed around the shelter.
There were **dozens of cats**.

"Hi!" said Tasha,
the manager.

“The cats need to get used to being with people. Can you play with them?” Tasha asked.

Hana **nodded**.

Hana combed the cats and played with them. She hatched a new plan ... to have a kitten sleepover!

Dad **sneezed**.

"Mum and Gemma won't be pleased," said Dad.

"They'll change their minds," said Hana. "Cosmo and Midnight are so cute!"

But ...

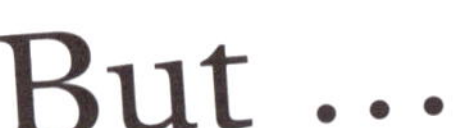

Cosmo gnawed and wrestled with Gemma's wool.

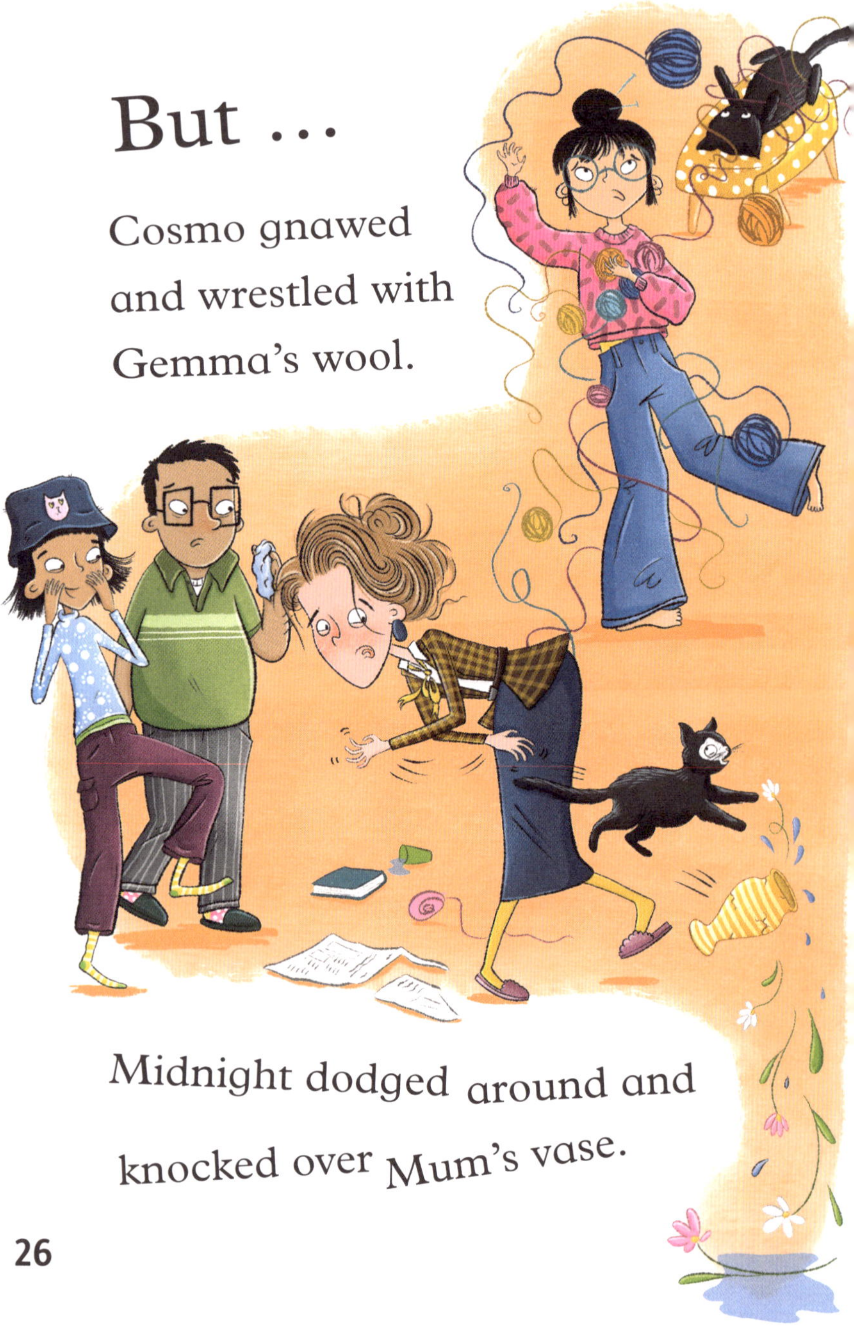

Midnight dodged around and knocked over Mum's vase.

"They're too **WILD** for our household," said Mum. "Besides, cats make Dad sneeze!"

The following week, Hana asked to take Raja home for a trial.

But ...

Raja behaved like he was the king of the castle.

He sneered at cat food, and gobbled Hana's shrimp.

When Gemma practised recorder, Raja's fur **BRISTLED** and he yowled. Dad winced.

Hana put Raja gently into his carry-case and fastened the clasp.

"You'll find a forever home soon," she sighed.

As time passed, Cosmo, Midnight and even Raja were adopted. It made Hana sad, but she kept helping at the shelter. She learned **everything** she could about cats.

When her family suggested other pets, she changed the subject.

One day when Hana was clearing a ledge, she noticed something. The cat cave was **wobbling**.

She kneeled and peered in. Something gazed back from within the shadows. Hana **gasped**.

"That is Cleo. She's a hairless cat," said Tasha.

Over the next few weeks, Hana was patient with Cleo. She talked to her all day in a gentle voice.

Slowly, Cleo became braver. At the shelter Christmas party, she even let Gemma stroke her wrinkled skin.

"How sweet!" said Mum. "It's a pity cats make Dad sneeze."

"Cleo is less likely to make people sneeze. This is because she's almost hairless," said Tasha.

It was Hana's **BEST** Christmas ever!

Look back

1 Why was Hana not allowed to have a cat?

2 What went wrong when she took cats home?

3 How did Hana manage to get a pet cat in the end?

In this book, you can find out lots of facts about cats!

STOP AND THINK

What do you know about cats?
What would you like to find out?

Hana's Book of Cat Facts

Written by Mio Debnam

Illustrated by Jennifer Jamieson

Contents

Cats!

Cats are common household pets, but they are **FAR** from ordinary.

Read on for some **surprising** and **interesting** facts!

DID YOU KNOW?

Cats like Cleo have some things in common with lions.

Nose prints

DID YOU KNOW?

Cats have nose prints. You can see them if they press their nose to glass.

No two cats have the same nose print! They are all **different**, just like human fingerprints!

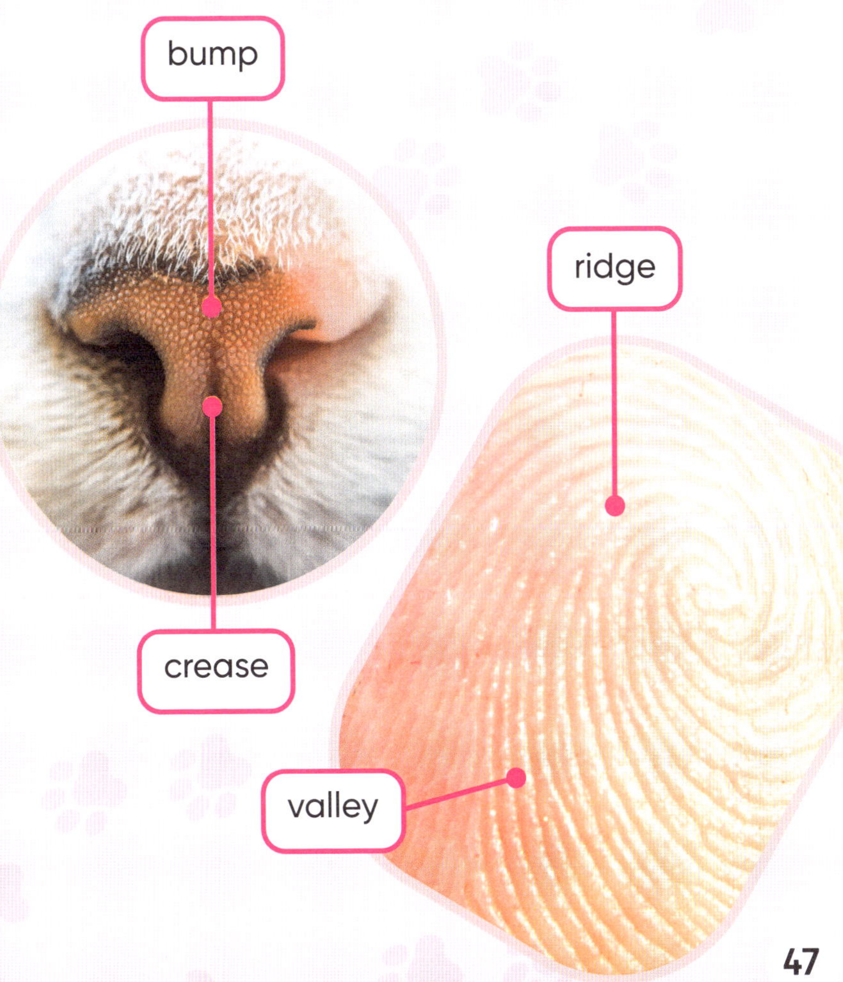

Climbing claws

Everyone knows cats are really good at climbing ... so why do some get **STUCK** in trees?

Cats' claws are like hooks. They allow cats to hold on and climb up trees, to dodge danger.

FUN FACT!

Cats can **retract** their claws, to protect the sharp tips.

Cats *can't* climb down headfirst. Their **hooked** claws would be facing the wrong way to hold them up.

Cats *can* climb down tail first.

However, some cats don't know how and get **STUCK!**

Communication

Kittens and mother cats **communicate** by meowing.

Adult cats rarely meow to each other. Instead, they communicate with their bodies.

DID YOU KNOW?

Adult cats hiss and purr to each other.

Adult pet cats meow to humans to help us understand them.

Running

Have you ever watched a cat run? If you have, you know that they can run very *fast!*

A cat's spine is very **flexible.** Cats bend and *stretch* out their backs as they run. This allows them to spring and take really long strides.

Grooming

Cats lick their fur to comb out **tangles**. This also gets rid of loose hairs, fleas and dead skin.

Cats spend around a **third** of their time grooming themselves. That's a lot of fur-licking!

FUN FACT!

Big cats, like tigers, groom themselves in a similar way!

Licking spreads the cat's **saliva** over its fur and skin. The saliva helps to clean the fur.

This is why a healthy cat isn't normally **smelly!**

Keeping cool

When it's hot, humans sweat to cool off. Cats have other ways to stay cool.

Cats **don't** sweat under their fur. Instead, they lick themselves. The saliva helps cool them down.

Cats can sweat from their paw-pads. If you see wet paw-prints, it's a sign the cat is **very hot!**

Cats also **pant** to cool down ... but the best option is to find a shady place to rest!

This lion is panting.

Sight

Cats are **really good** at noticing motion. However, they can't see things close up or far away very clearly.

Cats can see six times better than humans in the dark. However, they can't see as many tints!

Big cats

Big cats, like lions, are very similar to pet cats. They're excellent hunters and spend ages grooming! All cats like rubbing up against things, too.

jaguar

lion

puma

lynx

tiger

FUN FACT!

Your cat rubs its smell onto you. That's how other cats know who you belong to!

So the next time you see a cat, watch carefully. It's like a real-life wildlife **documentary**!

Glossary

communicate: to pass on a message

documentary: a film that tells you about real-life events

flexible: easy to bend or stretch

retract: pull back (to pull claws back into the paws)

saliva: spit

Index

Which day of the week do cats love the most?

Caturday